HOW TO DISCONNECT

SELF-DESTRUCTIVE

BEHAVIOR

10 STEPS TO PERSONAL POWER

TARA LARAE

DEDICATION

To my children Monté, Dominique and D'aunte. May this book remind you that you control your destiny by every choice you make. Balance is key. I am extremely proud of each one of you! I am grateful God choose me to be your mother.

CONTENTS

PREFACE

This book was inspired to help people get UNSTUCK! Self-sabotage is a very low frequency of self-respect, which makes it difficult to tap into self-love.

I did not realize I struggled with self-sabotage until my late 30s. It's super weird! I would be an overachiever in one aspect; on the other, I would start something and not finish it for no good reason. I would quit something when one thing went wrong because, in my head, it was about to be a snowball effect again, and I did not have the mental bandwidth to deal with it. I would allow the views of others to dictate my end result because I was looking for approval, and the sad part is that they were not in any position to offer it. Or how about dimming my light because I did not feel I deserved it?

I am sure many of us are damaged in some way or form. Some more than others, but not damaged beyond repair. In my opinion, self-sabotage comes from something that happened in the past.

For me, I do not know if it came from my parent's divorce at the tender age of seven. They both loved me so much, but somehow in the midst of fighting over me, they sometimes forgot about me. Or could it be family situations that I had to deal with? I still cannot talk about them today because that is not what black families do. It could possibly be me finding out I was pregnant at 17 with twins. College brochures quickly turned into prenatal brochures.

So, I figured it is time to put some action steps in place and do the work that would re-wire our daily activities and thoughts to create our own destiny. Why should we sit back and allow life to happen to us when we can be proactive and happen to it?

How to Use This Book:

1. Sequential Read with Reflection:

- Read the book from start to finish to get a complete overview. After your initial read-through, revisit the book, focusing this time on completing the action steps provided at the end of each chapter to deepen your understanding and application of the material.

2. Targeted Implementation:

- Read the book from beginning to end on your first pass. As you read, note the chapters that resonate most with you or seem immediately applicable. Once you've finished, return to these selected chapters and begin to implement the ideas and strategies they discuss.

3. Interest-Led Exploration:

- Begin by reading the Preface to understand the book's goals and structure. Then, review the Table of Contents to identify the chapters that immediately capture your interest. Start your reading with these chapters, allowing your curiosity and relevance to guide your exploration of the book's content.

These methods are designed to accommodate different reading styles and needs, ensuring that you can engage with and benefit from the book in a way that best suits you.

"The true beauty of this journey lies in its uniqueness — it's wholly yours. You have the wonderful opportunity to craft a path that resonates deeply with you, free from external distractions and influences. This is your moment, your choice, your journey.

I'm so proud of you for taking this step towards nurturing and honoring yourself through self-care. You're doing something truly commendable.

STEP 1:

ADMIT TO YOURSELF

Admitting to yourself that you engage in self-sabotage is a crucial first step in your journey to healing and growth. It requires courage and honesty to recognize the moments where you sabotaged your own success, whether through procrastination, negative self-talk, or by not honoring your needs and boundaries. This acknowledgment is about gaining clarity and understanding that these behaviors are protective mechanisms, and you should have compassion for yourself as you move forward with the readiness to change.

Once you have identified your patterns, it's crucial to approach them with kindness rather than criticism. Love yourself. Understand that your self-sabotaging behaviors are not a reflection of your capability or your worth but rather a reaction to past experiences. This shift in perspective allows you to manage those actions and replace them with strategies that support your success and growth. It is time for you to be intentional, take charge, and create new habits.

Doing so will open you up to a road towards self-empowerment and success.

Action Step:

Carry a small notebook, take notes on your phone, or use a digital app to record situations where you think you might have engaged in self-sabotage. Note the situation, your feelings at the time, and what you think may have triggered your behavior. Review your entries at the end of the week to identify patterns and triggers. This self-observation is pivotal in developing awareness and sets the foundation for transformative change.

SELF-REFLECTION

Write down how you feel after reading Step 1. This is just for you. It does not have to be constructed correctly. This is for you to catch your organic feelings.

Date:______________

____

____

____

____

____

____

____

____

____

____

____

____

STEP 2:

UNDERSTANDING THE WHY

Understanding WHY your self-sabotage is crucial in reversing the patterns. Start by writing down specific instances where you have noticed self-sabotaging behavior from the past in different areas of your life, home, work, and relationships. Identify three past events where you procrastinated on an important project at work, neglected household responsibilities, or withdrew emotionally from a partner during a disagreement. These actions may seem small; however, they can significantly stunt your growth in your personal and professional circle and have a heavy weight on your emotional well-being.

Reflect on each situation honestly and consider what triggered your self-sabotaging behavior. Was it fear of failure? A desire to avoid conflict or feelings of inadequacy which triggered a defense mechanism? Acknowledging these triggers is your first step towards change. For each instance, think about how you could have acted differently. Maybe instead of procrastinating, you could have broken the project into manageable tasks and set clear deadlines for each one. At home, you can set a daily reminder to complete chores or share responsibilities with family members to prevent feeling overwhelmed. In your relationship, instead of withdrawing from that person, perhaps a proactive approach of communicating your feelings through a letter would have been more constructive to get you point access. Make sure you request a response in the same manner, through a letter.

Action Step:

Create a Behavior Modification Plan. Use a journal to list each self-sabotaging event, its trigger, and a positive alternative action. Commit to implementing these alternative actions the next time you face similar circumstances. Review this journal weekly to assess your progress and adjust your strategies as necessary. This ongoing practice will not only help you become more aware of your patterns but also empower you to make consistent, positive changes in your behavior.

BEHAVIOR MODIFICATION PLAN

Use this behavior modification plan to log each self-sabotaging event. Take note of the event, what triggered you/the event, and a positive alternate action.

Date:______________

Self-Sabotage Event	Trigger	Positive Action

STEP 3:

TAKE FULL RESPONSIBILITY

Taking full responsibility for your thoughts and actions is pivotal in overcoming self-sabotage. This step involves a profound acknowledgment that your life is entirely yours to manage. Each decision you make shapes your future. It requires a shift from seeing yourself as a passive recipient of circumstances to becoming an active participant in your own life. Moving beyond blaming external conditions or other people for your setbacks is crucial. Instead, focus on your internal power and how you can influence your own outcomes. This transition involves recognizing the habitual patterns that no longer serve you and taking deliberate steps to change them.

Embracing responsibility means acknowledging your ability to change your behaviors, make healthier choices, and create the life you desire. This realization opens the door to genuine self-improvement and personal empowerment. It is about creating a mindset where you believe in your own strength and the possibility of change. By assuming full responsibility, you pave the way for personal growth and the development of resilience against future challenges. This mindset not only improves your personal life but also enhances your interactions with others as you begin to respond more constructively to difficult situations.

Action Step:

Implement writing a Responsibility Reflection. Every evening, reflect on the decisions you made that day. Write down at least one decision where you successfully took responsibility and one where you could have taken more. Assess what led to each decision and how you can improve. This routine will help you become more aware of how often you take responsibility for your life and encourage proactive behavior. Regularly reviewing your actions will help you foster a stronger sense of personal accountability and empowerment.

RESPONSIBILITY REFLECTION

Box A: Recall one time you took responsibility.

Box B: Recall a time you could have taken more.

Box C: What led to your decision above?

Box D: How can you improve from the answer above?

Box A	Box B

Box C	Box C

Box D	Box D

STEP 4:

CHANGE YOUR THOUGHT PROCESS

Allowing yourself to change your thought process is essential for personal growth and overcoming self-destructive habits. Our thoughts shape our reality; negative patterns can trap us in a cycle of self-doubt and missed opportunities, while positive thinking opens the door to potential and progress. By challenging and changing these patterns, you actively influence your feelings and behaviors, which leads to improved outcomes. This transformation doesn't happen overnight but requires a consistent effort to question and adjust the narratives you have believed about yourself and your capabilities.

Altering your thought process can significantly improve your mental and emotional well-being. Having negative thought patterns such as self-criticism or self-sabotage can lead to stress and depression. By consciously adopting a more positive and realistic way of thinking, you begin to see challenges as opportunities for growth rather than obstacles. This proactive mindset encourages resilience and a more fulfilling engagement with the world around you. It is about empowering yourself to navigate life's ups and downs with a stronger, more adaptable outlook.

Action Step:

Practice Thought Stopping and Replacement. Start by identifying a negative thought that frequently crosses your mind. Each time this thought arises, consciously say "stop" in your mind or aloud and replace it with a positive alternative. For example, replace thoughts like "I can't handle this" with "I can handle this by taking one step at a time." Keep a journal to track these changes and observe how they influence your mood and decisions over time. This method will help you develop a habit of mindful thinking and increase your mental agility.

SELF-REFLECTION

Write down how you feel after reading Step 1. This is just for you. It does not have to be constructed correctly. This is for you to catch your organic feelings.

Date:___________

____

____

____

____

____

____

____

____

____

____

____

____

STEP 5:

RECOGNIZE THAT YOU ARE WORTH THE EFFORT!

Recognizing you are worth the effort is fundamental in maintaining balance and fulfillment in all areas of your life. Often, we pour our energy into our work, family, friends, and community, striving to meet and exceed the expectations and needs of others. While this dedication is commendable, it's crucial to remember that your own needs are just as important. By investing in yourself at least as much as you invest in others, you not only enhance your own well-being but also increase your capacity to support those around you while setting the bar of how you should be treated. Self-care and personal development are not acts of selfishness; they are essential practices that enable you to be your best self for everyone, including you.

Putting effort into your own growth and happiness fosters healthy self-esteem and a more resilient mindset, which are both vital during challenging times. When you value yourself and acknowledge your worth, you're more likely to engage in activities that promote your well-being and reject those situations and people that may harm it. This can lead to healthier choices, such as pursuing interests that ignite your passion, seeking relationships that uplift you, and establishing boundaries that protect your energy. The belief that you deserve your own time and attention is empowering and can transform the way you interact with the world, making you a more grounded and confident individual.

Action Step:

Schedule Regular Self-Check-ins. Dedicate at least one hour each week to assess how well you're caring for yourself across various aspects of life: physical, emotional, and mental. During these check-ins, ask yourself if you are putting as much effort into your personal development as you are into your responsibilities and relationships. Use this time to plan activities that contribute to your growth and well-being, such as starting a new hobby, practicing meditation, or setting educational goals. Regular self-assessment ensures that you remain committed to your self-worth and continually make space for your needs and aspirations. Your life is valuable. We only get one. That makes it rare and, in turn, makes it priceless.

AFFIRMATIONS

Think of some affirmations or positive words just for you. Write them in this jar. Read this at least 5 times a day.

PAUSE......TIME FOR MINDFULNESS

Find a Quiet Space:

Choose a quiet and comfortable spot where you will not be disturbed. This could be a corner of your home, a peaceful outdoor area, or any space where you feel relaxed.

Get Comfortable:

Sit or lay down in a comfortable position. You can use a cushion or chair to support your posture if you choose to sit. Make sure your body feels relaxed and at ease.

Set a Time Limit:

Decide on a duration for your meditation session. Beginners may start with just 5-10 minutes and gradually increase as they become more comfortable with the practice.

Focus on Your Breath:

Close your eyes and take a few deep breaths to center yourself. In through your nose.... hold for a few seconds... out through your mouth, slowly. Allow your breath to return to its natural rhythm. Focus your attention on the sensation of breathing; feel the air entering and leaving your body.

Be Present:

As you continue to breathe, gently bring your awareness to the present moment. Notice any thoughts, sensations, or emotions that arise, but try not to get caught up in them. Allow every thought and feeling to come and go without attachment. Observe them without judgment, and then gently guide your focus back to your breath. Allow the thoughts to pass through your mind.

Stay Relaxed:

If you find your mind wandering, gently guide it back to your breath or the present moment. Remember, it's normal for thoughts to arise during meditation. Simply acknowledge them and then gently return your focus to your breath.

End Mindfully:

When your meditation session is over, before opening your eyes, take a moment to reflect on how you feel. Notice any changes in your body, mind, or emotions. Then, slowly bring your awareness back to your surroundings.

Practice Regularly:

Consistency is key to experiencing the benefits of meditation. Aim to practice daily, even if it's just for a few minutes at a time. Over time, you'll develop greater mindfulness, inner peace, and clarity of mind.

Remember, there's no right or wrong way to meditate, so feel free to experiment and find what works best for you. The most important thing is to approach your practice with openness, curiosity, and kindness towards yourself.

STEP 6:

BELIEVE IN YOURSELF

Believing in yourself despite the obstacles you currently face or the errors you've made in the past is a testament to your resilience and strength. This self-belief is not just an optimistic disposition but a powerful foundation for your future. Every individual encounters challenges and setbacks; however, these hurdles do not define your capabilities or your worth. Instead, they serve as lessons that contribute to your growth and understanding. By maintaining faith in yourself, you shift your focus from what has gone wrong to what can be achieved. This mindset is crucial because it empowers you to navigate through difficulties with confidence and to seize opportunities for improvements that might otherwise be overlooked.

Moreover, believing in yourself influences how you approach your future. It ensures that past mistakes are viewed not as permanent stains but as stepping stones to greater wisdom and strength. This perspective is vital because it frees you from the burden of past imperfections, allowing you to approach new endeavors with a clear and hopeful vision. Your belief in your ability to succeed becomes a self-fulfilling prophecy: the more you trust in your potential, the more likely you are to achieve your goals, regardless of the complexity of the path ahead.

Action Step:

Create a "Belief Bio." Write a short biography that focuses on your strengths, successes, lessons learned, and aspirations. Include statements that reinforce your belief in your ability to overcome challenges and achieve your goals. Read this bio regularly, especially during times of doubt or when faced with new challenges. This document will serve as a personal reminder of your resilience and capability to reinforce your self-belief and motivate you to keep pushing forward.

Practice Affirmation Recitals: Start and end your day with affirmations that focus on your strengths and goals. Choose or create affirmations that resonate deeply with you, such as "I am capable of achieving whatever I set my mind to" or "I trust in my ability to overcome challenges." Say these affirmations out loud in front of a mirror or write them down in a journal. This practice helps reinforce a positive self-image and strengthens your belief in your abilities.

SELF-REFLECTION

Belief "Bio".

Date:___________

STEP 7:

PROMISE TO END SABOTAGE

This step is crucial because it shifts your internal narrative from limitation to capability and possibility. When you make a firm commitment to end self-sabotage, you start to build a foundation of self-respect and self-worth. This change in self-perception is essential for personal development. It encourages you to make choices that support your well-being and success. This promise helps cultivate resilience as you learn to recognize and overcome the habitual responses that no longer serve you. You begin to understand that you are in control of your behavior and responses, which is empowering and transformative.

Making a promise to yourself to end self-sabotage is a powerful act of commitment that sets the stage for personal growth and success. This promise is more than just a decision; it's a pact that prioritizes your well-being and future. It reflects a deep recognition of the harm that self-sabotaging behaviors cause, not only to your goals but to your self-esteem and overall happiness. By committing to stop these behaviors, you affirm your worth and take control of your life's narrative. This commitment helps create a mental and emotional boundary against negative habits, empowering you to act in your best interest and align your actions with your aspirations. By consciously committing to stop these patterns, you signal to both your conscious and subconscious mind that you are ready to break free from these limiting behaviors.

Action Step:

Relax and write a heartfelt commitment letter to yourself detailing three things: 1. Explain why you want to stop self-sabotaging. 2. Describe what you hope to achieve by doing so. 3. Explain how your life will improve as a result. Sign the letter and place it somewhere you can see it daily, such as your desk, mirror, or personal journal. Whenever you feel tempted to fall back into old patterns, read the letter to remind yourself of the commitment you made and why it's important to you. This physical and symbolic gesture can reinforce your promise and keep you focused on your goals.

Date of commitment__________

Dear _________________

STEP 8:

RENEW YOUR COMMITMENT

Renewing your commitment to yourself is vital in maintaining momentum on your self-improvement and personal growth journey. It serves as a regular reminder of your goals and the reasons behind them, reinforcing your dedication and motivation. By periodically reaffirming your commitment, you ensure that your actions remain aligned with your true intentions and values. This renewal process not only rejuvenates your resolve but also helps you to adjust your strategies in response to any new circumstances or insights, keeping your approach fresh and effective.

The renewal process allows reflection and adaptation to be part of your new journey. As you grow and evolve, so do your needs and aspirations. Renewing your commitment offers the opportunity to adjust your goals to better suit your current circumstances and the lessons you've learned along the way. Your approach of periodically reaffirming your goals will keep you from becoming outdated or misaligned with your true self, which can demotivate and deter progress. It reinforces your motivation and engagement with your goals, keeping them relevant and exciting. This ongoing commitment is crucial for maintaining momentum and ensuring your efforts continue leading you towards fulfillment and success.

Action Step:

Schedule Regular Reflection Sessions. Set aside time each month for a reflection session where you assess the progress towards your goals and the effectiveness of your strategies. Use this time to celebrate successes, learn from setbacks, and identify any adjustments needed. During these sessions, consciously renew your commitment by writing down your renewed pledges and the reasons behind them. This written record can serve as both a motivational tool and a reminder of your ongoing journey, helping to keep your goals clear and your commitment strong.

MONTHLY PLANNER

Month:

Year:

SUN	MON	TUE	WED	THU	FRI	SAT

TOP PRIORITIES

NOTES

STEP 9:

KEEP AT IT. PERSEVERANCE IS KEY

Perseverance is a critical component of success in any endeavor. The journey to achieving significant goals is rarely straightforward or easy; it often involves encountering unexpected challenges and enduring setbacks. The resilience to continue despite these difficulties is what differentiates those who realize their aspirations from those who fall short. This consistent effort over time allows you to build the skills, knowledge, and experience necessary to overcome obstacles. More importantly, it cultivates an attitude of determination and grit, which are invaluable traits not just for specific projects but for life in general.

Maintaining your effort and focus over the long haul reinforces your commitment to your goals and boosts your confidence as you make incremental progress. Each small step forward, even if it's just a minor victory, is a testament to your dedication and a building block for future success. By keeping at it, you embed your pursuits into your identity, transforming them from mere tasks to integral parts of your self-concept. This identity reinforcement makes the pursuit of your goals an ongoing process, which naturally integrates into your daily habits and routines, thereby increasing the likelihood of achieving lasting results. As you apply these steps to your daily routine/thought process, you will be amazed at the difference you achieve and how much better your world outlook becomes!

Set Regular Review Sessions:

Schedule weekly or monthly review sessions for yourself to assess your progress towards your goals. Use these sessions to reflect on three things:

1. What have you accomplished?
2. What challenges you've faced?
3. What adjustments might be necessary to continue with forward movement?

This consistent review keeps your goals fresh in your mind and allows you to see the bigger picture, helping you stay motivated and focused even when progress seems slow. It is also an opportunity to celebrate successes, which can provide an emotional boost, reinforce your commitment, and motivate your spirit to continue.

"THERE IS

NO

EXPANSION

IF YOU

QUIT."

@innergizHER

STEP 10:

CONSIDER SEEKING PROFESSIONAL HELP

Considering professional help when your own efforts to change are proven ineffective is a wise and courageous step towards self-improvement.

Sometimes, the patterns embedded within us are rooted deep and complex, which could stem from past experiences or environmental factors that are difficult to unravel alone. Professionals such as counselors, therapists, life coaches, or social workers provide tools, strategies, and support to help you navigate complex emotions, behaviors, and situations. Seeking their assistance is not a sign of weakness but a proactive approach to taking charge of your mental health and well-being, ensuring you receive the support necessary to move forward effectively.

Moreover, there should be no shame in seeking professional help, just as there is no shame in seeking a doctor for a medical issue. Mental and emotional challenges are just as real and can be just as important as physical ones. Society's stigma around mental health is fading as more people recognize that mental wellness is a vital component of overall health. Seeking help not only benefits you but also sets a positive example for others who may be hesitant to seek help themselves. It contributes to a healthier, more understanding, and safer community.

Action Step:

If you need additional help, take your time to research and choose a professional. Start by identifying what kind of support you need — whether it's for mental health, career guidance, relationship counseling, or personal development. Look for qualified professionals in your area of choice, and check their credentials and reviews. Many professionals offer a free initial consultation, so take advantage of this to see if their approach aligns with your needs. Due to medical insurance understanding the importance of mental health, more of them cover the cost, so make sure you check with your insurance company. If you can outline what you hope to achieve through therapy or coaching, write it down. Also, write down any specific behaviors or patterns you want to change and any goals you wish to accomplish with their guidance. Having a clear set of objectives will help you communicate your needs more effectively during initial consultations and help the professional understand how best to assist you. If you are not at the step yet, that is fine. Just show up, and they will help you right where you are.

Congratulations!! You have made it through half the book! I think this would be a great time to take a break and reflect on the things you have learned about yourself. It is time for mindfulness through the art of meditation.

ABOUT TARA LARAE

Meet Tara Larae, a beacon of resilience and warmth who proudly raised three beautiful souls amidst the breathtaking backdrop of the San Francisco Bay Area. Tara's journey from teen motherhood to empowerment is a testament to the human spirit's capacity for growth and redemption.

Tara's quest for self-discovery began amidst the hallowed halls of the University of California, Berkeley, where she pursued her passion for understanding human dynamics, earning a Bachelor of Arts in Sociology and a Minor in Early Childhood Development. Little did she know, her academic pursuits would pave the way for a deeper exploration of her own inner landscape.

At the tender age of 17, Tara faced her most daunting challenge yet: the unexpected arrival of twin blessings (Boy/Girl). Suddenly thrust into adulthood, she found herself grappling with self-doubt and societal pressures that threatened to overshadow her inherent worth. Yet, with each obstacle she encountered, Tara emerged stronger, her spirit unbroken, her resolve unwavering.

As Tara matured, she embarked on a journey of self-acceptance and empowerment, refusing to be confined by the labels society often imposes on young mothers.

In "Finding Strength in the Journey," Tara Larae extends a heartfelt invitation to readers to join her on a transformative odyssey. Through candid storytelling and raw vulnerability, she shares the highs and lows of her personal evolution, offering solace and inspiration to those who may find themselves grappling with similar challenges. Tara's message is one of hope and resilience, a reminder that no matter how daunting life's obstacles may seem, victory is always within reach.

9 798218 436773